Original title:

A Starry Winter

Author: Sara Säde

ISBN HARDBACK: 978-9916-79-885-0

ISBN PAPERBACK: 978-9916-79-886-7

ISBN EBOOK: 978-9916-79-887-4

Chronicles of Snow and Stars

In the hush of night, whispers fall,
Snowflakes dance, a crystal thrall.
Stars above twinkle so bright,
Guardians of this winter night.

Footprints lost in white expanse,
Dreams entwined in snowy dance.
Moonlight kisses every flake,
Nature's breath, a gentle wake.

Frosty breaths, a chill in air,
Silent woods, a tranquil fare.
Branches bow with soft embrace,
Time stands still in this embrace.

Echoes of laughter, children play,
Sliding down the hills of gray.
Joyful shouts, like candles bright,
Illuminating winter's night.

As dawn breaks, the colors blend,
Golden rays on snow descend.
A tale of wonder, pure and vast,
In the chronicles, winter's cast.

Memory of a Radiant Winter Night

Under stars, the world aglow,
A blanket soft with whispers slow.
Candles flicker, shadows play,
In this warmth, we drift away.

Frosted windows, patterns divine,
Each shape a memory, a sign.
Laughter echoes through the hall,
In our hearts, it binds us all.

The scent of pine, a sweet perfume,
Christmas lights dispel the gloom.
Together wrapped in love's embrace,
Radiance found in every space.

Hot cocoa waits, a tempting call,
By the fire, we gather all.
Stories shared from times long past,
In our hearts, these moments last.

Winds outside weave tales untold,
While embers fade, our dreams unfold.
Winter's magic, a fleeting light,
Preserved in memory, radiant night.

As snowflakes fall, we cherish deep,
The bonds we've forged that night to keep.
In the stillness, love's delight,
A radiant glow, our hearts take flight.

Dreams of Ice and Light

In the silence, whispers fall,
Icicles shimmer, standing tall.
Gentle frost on branches cling,
As winter's breath begins to sing.

Moonlit paths of silver glow,
Softly guiding through the snow.
Frigid air, a crisp delight,
Beneath the dreams of ice and light.

Arctic Skies

Stars are scattered, frozen bright,
Painting tales across the night.
In the depths of azure blue,
The arctic skies call out to you.

Whales beneath the icy swell,
In whispers deep, their stories dwell.
Glacial winds, a soft caress,
In nature's realm, we find our rest.

Glittering High

Mountains stand with crowns of white,
Sparkling crystals catch the light.
In lofty peaks, a vision clear,
Where dreams and earth seem to endear.

Echoes of the eagles' flight,
Soaring high, in bold delight.
With every breath, the world feels new,
A glittering path, our spirits flew.

Woven Dreams of Winter

Threads of snow in twilight spun,
Whispering secrets, one by one.
Each flake dances, a fleeting charm,
In winter's grip, we find our calm.

A tapestry of silence wide,
Where memories and hopes reside.
Beneath the frost, our hearts connive,
In woven dreams, we come alive.

Celestial Crystals Above

Glimmers flicker in the dark,
Celestial notes of nature's spark.
A symphony beneath the stars,
Eternal lovers, near and far.

With every breath, the cosmos hums,
In quiet reverie, the magic comes.
Crystals twinkle while shadows play,
Guiding our dreams till break of day.

Wonder Beneath the Frozen Sky

Amidst the frost, a silence lies,
Whispers dance where snowflakes rise.
Beneath the chill, a secret hum,
Nature speaks, though winter's come.

Stars above in crystal light,
Shimmer softly through the night.
Magic lingers in the air,
A wondrous world, both bright and rare.

Trees adorned with icy lace,
Majesty in every space.
Footsteps crunch on frozen ground,
In this stillness, peace is found.

Breath like fog in cold embrace,
Time stands still in this shared place.
The beauty found in every breath,
Life persists through winter's depth.

In the heart of winter's reign,
Hope awakens, breaking chain.
Wonder shines beneath the sky,
A promise whispered—never die.

Luminescence in the Cold

Night descends, a canvas wide,
Beneath the stars, we dare to glide.
Frosty breath paints the air,
Illusions spark, a dreamer's flair.

Crystals twinkle on the ground,
In this beauty, love is found.
Moonlight bathes the world in glow,
Whispers only winter knows.

Frozen streams begin to hum,
Melodies from shadows come.
Each step echoes, crisp and clear,
In this quiet, magic's near.

Wind carries tales of old,
Secrets of the night unfold.
Every flake, a wish that's spun,
Underneath the watching sun.

With every breath, we feel alive,
In the cold, our hopes derive.
Laughing voices, bright and bold,
A dance of warmth in winter's hold.

Secrets Wrapped in Winter's Embrace

Snowflakes whisper on the breeze,
Cocooned in silence, heart's at ease.
Branches bow in purest grace,
Winter wraps in soft embrace.

Glistening trails where creatures roam,
Marking paths to find a home.
Each footprint speaks of stories past,
In frost, the echoes ever last.

The quiet hum of unseen life,
Woven deep amid the strife.
Nature holds its secrets tight,
Cradled in the cloak of night.

As icy breath caresses trees,
Winter carries softest pleas.
For every heart that seeks a way,
Hope reawakens with the day.

In the chill, a warmth turns bright,
Revealing dreams wrapped in the night.
Together, under stars, we find,
A bond that time cannot unwind.

Glacial Dreams and Starlit Streams

Frozen rivers gently flow,
Underneath the moonlit glow.
Glacial dreams take flight on air,
Wandering souls lost in prayer.

Stars like jewels, bright and bold,
Scatter stories yet untold.
From the ice, a spirit calls,
In the silence, magic falls.

Cool winds carry softest sighs,
Bringing whispers from the skies.
Each breath mingled with the night,
Promises of dawn's first light.

Nature hums a lullaby,
As shadows dance and wonders fly.
In the stillness, truth awakes,
A fragile world that gently shakes.

With every heartbeat, dreams expand,
In glacial grasp, we understand.
Together, we embrace the flow,
In starlit streams, our spirits grow.

The Beauty of Frosted Moments

Crystals dance on winter's breath,
Whispers of beauty, life bequeath.
Silvery veils on branches cling,
Nature's art, a quiet spring.

Moments frozen in time's embrace,
Glistening jewels upon each place.
In the stillness, secrets unfold,
A tapestry of magic, bold.

Every flake, a fleeting wish,
Transforming earth in frosted swish.
The world adorned in white's soft hue,
A wonderland, forever new.

Footprints left in powdery delight,
Sharing tales of the silent night.
Each breath a cloud against the chill,
In this beauty, hearts do thrill.

Glittering Beneath the Dark

Stars like diamonds in the void,
Whispered secrets, dreams deployed.
Night enfolds in velvet grace,
Shadows dance in endless space.

A universe of silent sighs,
Glistening echoes, ancient ties.
Each flicker tells a tale untold,
Of love and loss, of brave and bold.

The moon, a guardian from above,
Illuminates the night with love.
Darkness wears a sparkling crown,
In every heart, hope's softly sown.

Through the stillness, wishes soar,
Finding light forevermore.
In shadows deep, we make our mark,
Glittering dreams beneath the dark.

Stardust on Our Breath

In whispers soft, we trace the sky,
With stardust dreams, we learn to fly.
Each heartbeat echoes through the night,
Carrying wishes, burning bright.

Our laughter mingles with the stars,
A symphony of cosmic bars.
Dancing through the void, we roam,
Finding in space our shared home.

Moments stitched with threads of light,
We journey forth into the night.
With every breath, the cosmos sings,
Of love and life, and simple things.

In the silence, magic stirs,
A universe within us purrs.
With stardust on our breath, we soar,
To distant worlds, forevermore.

Cosmic Frost

In the chill of interstellar night,
Frost takes form, a shimmering sight.
Galaxies twinkle, their breath so cold,
Whispers of wonders yet untold.

Stars weave patterns in the dark,
Each flicker, a journey, a spark.
The universe cloaked in frosty grace,
A silent dance, a glowing embrace.

Cosmic winds brush against our skin,
Emerald dreams where journeys begin.
Frosted echoes, sweet and divine,
Time stands still in this sacred line.

In the depths of the night, we find,
Beauty that stirs the restless mind.
Cosmic frost, our hearts ignite,
Joining the stars in endless flight.

Secret Nightfall

Beneath the cloak of darkened skies,
Whispers of dreams begin to rise.
Shadows dance in the pale moonlight,
Lost in the arms of tranquil night.

Silent stars twinkle with delight,
Guiding the wishes taking flight.
Every breath feels like a sigh,
As the world breathes, slow and shy.

Glimmers of hope in the still air,
Softly weaving a tale of care.
Night's embrace cradles the day,
As twilight's glow begins to sway.

In secret realms where silence plays,
Time gently bends and softly stays.
Nightfall holds a magic so grand,
In the darkness, dreams take a stand.

With every heartbeat, joy expands,
Under the moon's enchanting hands.
The night retreats with softest grace,
Leaving echoes in a quiet space.

The Celestial Veil

A veil of stars upon the sea,
Shimmering secrets, wild and free.
Soft whispers ride the morning light,
Painting the canvas of new sight.

Clouds drift softly, a gentle dance,
In the vast sky, a fleeting chance.
Color spills as the dawn breaks through,
Awakening dreams that feel so new.

In the twilight glow, shadows play,
Carving stories in gold and gray.
Each breath cradles the earth's sweet song,
As day unfolds, where all belong.

With cosmic tales forever spun,
Under the watchful, timeless sun.
Threads of stardust weave the night,
In this realm where dreams take flight.

From high above, the heavens gleam,
In every heart, a whispered dream.
The celestial veil will always stay,
Wrapping the world in a soft sway.

Wonders in the Hushed Night

In the stillness where shadows creep,
Life holds its breath, in silence deep.
Stars sprinkle glitter upon the ground,
In this moment, magic is found.

Soft sighs of the night wind weave,
Every rustle seems to believe.
Under the moon's gentle caress,
Time stands still, free from distress.

Crickets sing in a soft refrain,
Echoing dreams, a sweetened pain.
Night blooms brightly, a fragrant song,
Whispering secrets to those who long.

The world transformed in shades of blue,
With each moment, something feels new.
A canvas of dreams begins to paint,
Life's hidden wonders, without restraint.

Through the dark, a soft glow shines,
Illuminating hidden designs.
In the hush of night, hearts unite,
Wonders waiting in soft moonlight.

Resonance of the Frosted Sky

Beneath the frost where whispers meet,
A frozen tale beneath our feet.
Cold air wraps the earth's gentle spine,
Bringing the chill of a world divine.

Each star hangs like frost on a thread,
Guiding the dreams in soft beds.
Infinite wonders in silence grow,
Echoing life beneath the snow.

The earth sleeps under a winter's shroud,
Wrapped in stillness, dreamers proud.
Silvery glimmers like tiny seas,
Floating softly upon the breeze.

With every breath, the night feels clear,
Crystals shimmering, drawing near.
In this silence, we hear the bliss,
Of a world that wakes with a gentle kiss.

As dawn approaches, colors arise,
Painting warmth in the frosted skies.
The resonance of night will fight,
To keep our dreams close, holding tight.

Night's Whispering Glow

In shadows deep, the silence falls,
A lantern's light through twilight calls.
The moon unfolds her silver lace,
As whispers dance in night's embrace.

Dreams take flight on gentle breeze,
While stars conspire through rustling leaves.
Each twinkle holds a secret tale,
As night envelops, soft and frail.

With every heartbeat, time stands still,
The world asleep, a tranquil thrill.
In starlit paths where shadows weave,
The night reveals what hearts believe.

With muffled steps, we wander slow,
In night's embrace, our spirits glow.
For in the stillness, beauty flows,
In every sigh of night's soft prose.

Soft Twinkles on Frosted Pines

Frosted boughs in moonlight gleam,
Soft twinkles whisper, nature's dream.
As winter's breath enchants the wood,
Each flake a marvel, pure and good.

Snowflakes dance on gentle air,
Like tiny jewels, rich and rare.
They quilt the earth in silvery hue,
A frosted wonder, fresh and new.

Pine trees stand like sentinels proud,
Garbed in beauty, nature's shroud.
With every crack of driven branch,
The forest breathes, a frosty dance.

In this stillness, hearts ignite,
Soft twinkles sparkle in the night.
A world transformed, so pure, so fine,
Frosted pines with twinkling shine.

Star-Kissed Snowflakes

As winter's breath begins to fall,
Star-kissed snowflakes dance and call.
Each flake a wish, a whispered prayer,
Caught in the stillness, light as air.

They twirl and glide through chilly night,
A frosty tapestry of white.
Beneath the glow of cosmic wonders,
Each drift a secret that softly thunders.

Like nature's jewels, they grace the ground,
A soft embrace, without a sound.
With every shimmer, stories grow,
In winter's spell, we come to know.

In every flurry, magic is found,
Within the hush, our souls are bound.
Star-kissed dreams in twilight's thrall,
In winter's dance, we feel it all.

Radiant Nights of Frost

Upon the hills, the frost does gleam,
Radiant nights in a wintry dream.
Each moment sparkles, crystal bright,
As stars sing soft through the velvet night.

The world is draped in a silken sheet,
Where shadows linger, calm and sweet.
In every corner, wonder glows,
While frosty breath through silence flows.

A hidden palette, pure delight,
Awaits the dawn, a hopeful flight.
In stillness wrapped, we find our way,
In radiant nights, forever stay.

Through frozen gardens, shadows creep,
In dreams awakened, softly seep.
With every heartbeat, hope ignites,
In these radiant, starry nights.

Celestial Frost

In the hush of winter's breath,
Stars blink like diamonds bright,
Frost whispers on silent nights,
Painting the world in silver light.

Moonlight dances on the snow,
Casting shadows soft and deep,
Each crystal glimmers in a row,
A tranquil secret, the earth must keep.

Glistening branches bow and sway,
Beneath the weight of icy lace,
Nature's art in cold array,
A serene and breathtaking space.

The air is crisp, the world anew,
Breath manifests in gentle clouds,
Every heartbeat feels so true,
In the quiet, joy enshrouds.

Celestial frost, a fleeting gift,
Moments wrapped in shimmering dreams,
As night begins its starry shift,
Every sparkle softly gleams.

Nightfall's Luminous Embrace

The sun dips low beneath the veil,
Night unfurls with silver grace,
Stars awaken, a brilliant tale,
In nightfall's luminous embrace.

Moonbeams cast a radiant glow,
Whispers of dreams glide through the trees,
A gentle wind begins to blow,
Bringing tales on nighttime breeze.

Shadows stretch and softly blend,
With echoes of a hidden song,
Amidst the stars, the world will mend,
In night's sweet arms, we all belong.

Crickets serenade the night,
Their harmony a soothing balm,
Every moment feels so right,
Wrapped in nature's tranquil calm.

As dawn approaches, soft and slow,
The sky blushes in hues anew,
But in our hearts, the night will glow,
In luminous embrace, forever true.

Whispers of the Frozen Sky

Underneath the azure dome,
Whispers float on icy air,
Clouds drift in a frosted roam,
Carrying secrets everywhere.

A chill that kisses cheeks so red,
Each breath a plume of ghostly grace,
Nature sings where angels tread,
In the stillness, dreams find place.

Stars twinkle in a velvet sea,
While moonlight strokes the frozen ground,
Each glimmer holds a mystery,
In silence, profound truths abound.

The world transformed, a glistening site,
Trees adorned like crystal towers,
In frozen whispers, hearts feel light,
Amongst the beauty's aching powers.

As the night drapes its soft cloak,
Frozen sky, a delicate sigh,
In its silence, dreams evoke,
Whispers of winter's lullaby.

Moonlit Dreams in Indigo

In the realm of twilight's sway,
Indigo skies begin to roam,
Moonlit dreams softly play,
Guiding lost hearts gently home.

Stars glimmer like wishes cast,
Over fields where shadows weave,
A tapestry till night has passed,
In ethereal hues, we believe.

The night air breathes a mystic song,
Coyote howls in the distance near,
Whispers of love, so profound,
In every echo we can hear.

Silhouettes dance beneath the light,
Blue petals float in midnight's stream,
Lost in dreams where hearts take flight,
In this realm, we dare to dream.

With every pulse, the world feels new,
In indigo's embrace, we find,
Moonlit visions, sweet and true,
In night's wonder, forever bind.

Frozen Night's Serenade

The moon hangs low in icy skies,
Whispers dance in shadowed sighs.
Stars like diamonds gleam and fade,
In this night, enchantment's laid.

Silence drapes the world so fine,
Snowflakes twirl in soft decline.
Nature breathes, a tranquil sound,
In frozen dreams, we're spellbound.

Glistening trees in silver coat,
Hearts feel light upon this mote.
A symphony of hush and grace,
In this moment, time's embrace.

Echoes of the past arise,
Through the chill, their spirits rise.
Whispers of a fleeting cheer,
Hold this night, forever near.

Canvas of Cold Light

Brushstrokes of frost on window panes,
Painting tales of winter's reigns.
A canvas wide with frigid hue,
Each glimmer speaks of cold and true.

Softly falling crystalline tears,
Filling hearts and silencing fears.
Nature's palette, stark yet bright,
A masterpiece of cold, pure light.

Horizon kissed by morning's breath,
Colors blend, a dance with death.
Life and stillness intertwine,
In this realm, all is divine.

Gentle whispers on the breeze,
Carried softly through the trees.
Fingers trace this artful scene,
Where every shade feels like a dream.

The Stillness of Celestial Nights

Waves of quiet kiss the land,
Where starlit dreams are gently planned.
Each twinkle holds a secret bright,
In the stillness of the night.

Cosmic breath, a tender sigh,
Beneath the vast, unending sky.
Heaven's canvas, dark and deep,
Cradles all in peaceful sleep.

Silent echoes drift on high,
While shadows weave and softly lie.
Moments linger, time stands still,
In this vast, enchanting thrill.

Infinite mysteries unfold,
Stories spun in threads of gold.
Stars bear witness, ancient light,
In the stillness of the night.

Winter's Ethereal Canvas

A tapestry of white and blue,
Each thread tells stories, fresh and new.
Mountains cloaked in shimmering frost,
In winter's grasp, we find what's lost.

Every flake, a fleeting grace,
Drawn in silence, a soft embrace.
Branches bow under the weight,
While the world holds its breath, so late.

Frosty whispers fill the air,
The magic lingers everywhere.
Nature sighs, a gentle cheer,
As winter paints, so crystal clear.

In every moment, wonder gleams,
Where imagination weaves its dreams.
Life finds beauty, pure and true,
In winter's gift, a vibrant view.

A Tale of Twinkling Snow

Amidst the quiet night,
Snowflakes dance in shimmering light.
Each one falls, a dream unfurled,
A gentle kiss upon the world.

Footprints trace a secret path,
Whispers echo, nature's laugh.
In the moon's embrace, we sigh,
Underneath the velvet sky.

Trees wear coats of sparkling white,
Blankets cover earth's delight.
Children's laughter fills the air,
Joy abounds, without a care.

Fireplaces crackle, glow,
Telling tales of long ago.
While cold winds softly play their tune,
Hearts are warmed beneath the moon.

In this hush of twilight's stay,
We find magic in the sway.
A tale of snow, so pure and bright,
In the quiet, endless night.

Veil of Winter's Wonder

A veil of frost on every bough,
Nature dons her crystal gown.
Whispers of the winter breeze,
Stir the stillness, chase the freeze.

Candles flicker, shadows dance,
Time slows down in this romance.
Underneath the starlit skies,
Hope awakens, softly flies.

Streams are silent, wrapped in sleep,
Secrets of the night we keep.
With every breath, the chill we feel,
A world reborn, a winter's reel.

Snowflakes twirling, soft and light,
Painting dreams in purest white.
Magic swirls in frosty air,
A moment cherished, beyond compare.

Veil of wonder, draped so fine,
Nature's art in every line.
In the quiet, pure and vast,
We find a beauty meant to last.

Phosphorescent Chills

A shimmer in the moonlit glow,
Nature's magic, soft and slow.
Silver frost on meadow's breath,
Whispers of impending death.

Chilled air wraps the earth in dreams,
Silence reigns as starlight beams.
Every shadow tells a tale,
Of winter's song, soft and pale.

Phosphorescent lights in the dark,
Draw our hearts with their sweet spark.
In the freeze, we find a warmth,
Guiding us through winter's charm.

Hidden paths, our secrets keep,
Underneath the snow, we sleep.
And in the stillness, dare to find,
The tender threads that bind mankind.

With every chill, a memory grows,
A tapestry of winter's prose.
Phosphorescent whispers call,
Reminding us that we are all.

Armour of Twilight's Glimmer

Twilight cloaks the fading day,
Wonders weave in muted play.
Shadows stretch and softly blend,
In this realm where dreams ascend.

Glimmers dance on icy streams,
In the hush, we weave our dreams.
Each star twinkles a shared wish,
In the silence, a tender bliss.

Armour of the night soon forms,
Wrapped in peace, the heart transforms.
Through the darkness, fireflies glow,
A gentle guide through winter's flow.

While the world begins to rest,
Hope ignites within the chest.
In the depths of chilly air,
Love ignites, a spark laid bare.

As twilight kisses the night sky,
Stars emerge, a soft goodbye.
In nature's arms, we find our way,
Armour of glimmer, come what may.

Silver Gleams on Silent Snow

Silver shines in moonlit night,
Softly falling, pure delight.
Whispers dance on frosty air,
Nature's beauty, rare and fair.

Footprints vanish, lost in white,
Shadows mingle, out of sight.
Blanket spreads, a tranquil scene,
Dreams awaken, calm and clean.

Crisp and quiet, time stands still,
Every heartbeat, winter's thrill.
Stars above begin to gleam,
Snowflakes drift, a silent dream.

Branches bow with crystal lace,
Frosted jewels in nature's grace.
Softly glows the world anew,
Silent night, a perfect view.

Beneath the sky, a world so bright,
Silver gleams on snow tonight.
A moment held, forever dear,
In winter's arms, I linger near.

Constellations in the Chill

Stars are scattered, bright and bold,
In the chill, their secrets told.
Silent whispers form a tale,
Of ancient light on icy veil.

Frosty breath on winter's night,
Guides my gaze to cosmic light.
Each twinkle holds a distant past,
A universe so vast, so vast.

Beneath this canvas, dreams ignite,
Constellations in the night.
Guiding hearts with shimmering grace,
In the dark, we find our place.

Snowflakes pause to catch a sight,
Of the galaxies shining bright.
In the cold, our spirits soar,
Finding magic at the core.

Underneath this starry dome,
In the chill, we find our home.
Every glimmer, every glow,
Whispers of the world below.

Midnight Radiance

Midnight whispers, soft and clear,
Radiance wraps the world so near.
Silver beams through trees so tall,
Casting shadows, a gentle call.

Glowing embers in the sky,
Stars like lanterns, floating high.
Every twinkle, soft embrace,
Illuminates the quiet space.

Silent moments fill the air,
Purest beauty, beyond compare.
Moonlight paints the ground with care,
A silver touch, beyond despair.

Breath of night, a tranquil sight,
Dancing echoes, taking flight.
In this calm, our worries cease,
In midnight's hold, we find our peace.

As the world begins to sleep,
Radiance vast, a secret deep.
In the silence, spirits rise,
Midnight dreams beneath the skies.

Frosted Twilight

Twilight settles, day departs,
Frosty breath in winter's arts.
Colors blend in softest hues,
Whispers dance on evening's muse.

Crimson skies to azure blue,
Frosted air that feels so true.
Gentle sighs of day's goodbye,
In this glow, the shadows lie.

Trees in silhouette stand tall,
Nature's wonders, a silent call.
Frosted leaves in twilight's glow,
Painting scenes in softest flow.

The world is hushed, a magic spell,
In the chill where dreamers dwell.
As twilight wraps its tender light,
Frosted magic fills the night.

In the stillness, hearts align,
Finding peace in dusk divine.
Frosted twilight, a sweet serenade,
Where memories and dreams are made.

Elysium of the Winter Dawn

The sky blushes with soft gold,
As silence wraps the sleeping world.
Whispers of light break the night,
In this calm, dreams take flight.

Snowflakes dance on frosty airs,
Crystals woven, nature's wares.
Each breath a mist, pure and bright,
Morning glows, banishing night.

Trees stand tall, cloaked in white,
Amidst the glow, a pure delight.
A tranquil heart in frigid grace,
Embraces peace in this embrace.

Footsteps crunch on frozen ground,
In every corner, beauty found.
Elysium's touch, a gentle hand,
In winter's realm, we make our stand.

From the mountains to valleys low,
Nature's art in every snow.
A frost-kissed world, so divine,
In winter's heart, we intertwine.

Aurora's Embrace in the Stillness

In the stillness of dawn's grace,
Auroras weave and softly trace.
Colors blend, a painted sky,
As nature breathes a gentle sigh.

Whispers dance on icy streams,
Echoing the night's cool dreams.
Stars begin to bid farewell,
In vibrant hues, their tales to tell.

Snowflakes twirl in magic's charm,
While winter wraps us in its arm.
An embrace both warm and cold,
In this moment, stories unfold.

The landscape glows, ethereal light,
Transforming dark to pure delight.
Silhouettes in frosty air,
Capturing beauty everywhere.

With every ray, our spirits soar,
In winter's grip, we seek for more.
Aurora's touch, a fleeting breath,
In the stillness, a dance with death.

Frost's Candid Glimpse

Frosted panes with stories told,
Glimmers of silver, shy and bold.
In every flake, a world anew,
Nature's canvas, every hue.

Candid glimpses through the trees,
A shiver carried by the breeze.
The earth wears white like a gown,
A tranquil beauty all around.

In quiet corners, shadows play,
As sunlight starts to greet the day.
Crystalline whispers in the air,
Invite us to pause, to care.

Each sparkle tells of winter's lore,
In this stillness, we explore.
Frost shines bright on every blade,
A brief moment that won't fade.

From dawn till dusk, the world awakes,
In every breath, the beauty shakes.
Frost's candid glimpse, a fleeting chance,
In winter's magic, we find our dance.

The Sparkle Beneath the Cold

Underneath the icy hold,
Lies a treasure, bright and bold.
Beneath the frost, life finds a way,
Whispers of hope in disarray.

Glimmers dance on frozen streams,
Echoes of forgotten dreams.
Silent songs the winter sings,
Of magic locked in frozen things.

Crystals shimmer in the light,
Reflecting hope in winter's night.
A world transformed, beauty untold,
Within the depths, the brave and bold.

The air is crisp, the heart is clear,
In this stillness, we draw near.
To the secret whispers of the cold,
Where dreams and stories intertwine and fold.

With every breath, the year unfolds,
In winter's heart, our magic molds.
The sparkle glows, a gentle spark,
Beneath the cold, igniting the dark.

Celestial Wishes in the Winter

In the hush of the night sky,
Stars whisper dreams so bright.
Frosted winds carry their tune,
Guiding wishes 'neath the moon.

Crystals twinkle in the trees,
Dancing softly in the breeze.
Each wish a spark, a gentle glow,
Fleeting moments, drifting slow.

Snowflakes fall, a quiet grace,
Painting worlds in white embrace.
In this stillness, hearts align,
Finding peace in the divine.

Glimmers spark the winter night,
As if the heavens ignite.
Celestial wonders fill the air,
In each breath, the magic's there.

Hope aflame in frosty air,
Winter's beauty, beyond compare.
In this season, dreams take flight,
Boundless wishes in the light.

Frozen Memories of the Cosmos

In the depths of winter's chill,
Memories linger, time stands still.
Galaxies captured in a frost,
Moments cherished, never lost.

Nebulas spun in crystal time,
Echoes of laughter, pure and prime.
Frozen whispers of the past,
Each star a tale, a fortune cast.

Comets trail through silent nights,
Guiding dreams with cosmic lights.
Every flake, a story told,
In silver hues, they shine like gold.

The universe, a canvas wide,
Where memories and hopes abide.
In the snowy depths we find,
A connection, intertwined.

As shadows dance and silence reigns,
Winter's grasp, a soft refrains.
In frozen dreams, we uncover
The cosmos calls, a whispered lover.

Dances of Light and Snow

Light cascades on fields of white,
Snowflakes twirl in joyous flight.
Nature's ballet, pure and clear,
A celebration drawing near.

Stars conspire in the night sky,
Frosty paths where spirits fly.
Each step a hymn, a soft embrace,
Tracing patterns in time and space.

Refracted beams in icicles,
Illuminating hidden miracles.
The world transforms, each flake unique,
In winter's grace, the silence speaks.

With every gust, the shadows sway,
As light and snow begin to play.
The universe takes center stage,
In this dance, we turn the page.

Twirling thoughts in winter's glow,
Memories drift like falling snow.
In this magic, hearts unite,
To witness dance, in pure delight.

Illuminated Silence

In the quiet of the night,
Silence sparkles, pure delight.
Stars are scattered, pure and bright,
Painting shadows with their light.

Crystalline whispers fill the air,
Holding secrets we all share.
Silent breaths in winter's fold,
Stories waiting to be told.

A frozen lake reflects the sky,
Mirroring dreams as time floats by.
Crickets cease, the world holds still,
In this pause, we feel the thrill.

Underneath the starry dome,
A sense of peace, we call it home.
Each twinkling gem, a wish in flight,
Guiding us through the soft twilight.

In the stillness, find your place,
Let the silence grace your space.
Illuminated moments bright,
Bathe your soul in winter's light.

Mysteries Beneath the Winter Canopy

Whispers in the falling snow,
Secrets that the shadows know.
Branches draped in crystal lace,
Conceal a world in quiet grace.

Footprints lead to hidden dreams,
Nature's hush, a softening theme.
Beneath the boughs, the silence swells,
Each breath a tale that winter tells.

Frosted leaves hold glimmers rare,
Patterns drawn with loving care.
Creeping vines in icy embrace,
Echo stories time can't erase.

Dancing shadows in the light,
Colors fade but spirits bright.
Mysteries within the frost,
Reveal the beauty found, not lost.

Every flake a whispered song,
In the quiet, we belong.
As dawn breaks on winter's reign,
Life awakens once again.

The Glowing Canvas Above

Stars twinkle in the vast expanse,
Guiding dreams in a cosmic dance.
Each glimmer paints a story bright,
A tapestry woven in the night.

Nebulas swirl in violet hues,
Whispers of ancient worlds we muse.
Celestial bodies drift and spin,
Letting our imaginations begin.

The moon, a lantern in the sky,
Illuminates shadows passing by.
Every twinkling spark a sign,
Mapping paths for hearts to align.

Constellations whisper lore,
Secrets hidden in cosmic core.
Echoes of light from realms afar,
A glowing canvas, our guiding star.

In stillness, we gaze, we ponder,
Feeling the magic, the infinite wonder.
Under this sky, we seek, we strive,
In the glow of the night, we are alive.

Celestial Tears on Frozen Mornings

Morning light brings icy tears,
Glistening drops of winter years.
Each one tells a silent tale,
Of beauty in the cold, so pale.

Sunrise paints the world anew,
Casting gold on the frosty dew.
As shadows stretch and softly fade,
Nature's quiet dreams are laid.

Breath is visible in the air,
Like whispers floating everywhere.
A heart beats in the crisp, cold dawn,
Awakening with the stretching lawn.

Trees adorned with diamonds bright,
Each branch a spark in morning light.
Frozen moments, fleeting art,
Crafted by the winter's heart.

Celestial tears, a wondrous gift,
Each drop a promise, spirits lift.
In every glimmer, hope remains,
Life anew, where love sustains.

Echoes of Frost

The world is still beneath the frost,
Whispers of warmth we count the cost.
Silence wraps the earth in white,
Echoes dance in the pale moonlight.

Footsteps crunch on icy trails,
Each sound a story that never fails.
Frosty breath, a fleeting kiss,
Moments cherished, we shan't miss.

Glistening branches sway and bend,
Nature's beauty, a lovely blend.
Winds carry tales of the unseen,
In frosty hues of silver sheen.

Echoes linger in the air,
Whispers of love, a quiet prayer.
Winter blooms in silence loud,
Beauty wrapped in a misty shroud.

Every dawn, a chance to find,
Echoes of frost that gently remind.
In this chill, there's warmth to hold,
A precious truth, a tale retold.

Glimmers in the Winter Breeze

Whispers of frost on the pines,
Glimmers dance in the twilight,
Cold air sings through the branches,
Stars peek through the shivering night.

Silver moonlight paints the ground,
Footsteps crunch on the frozen floor,
Silent peace in the quiet town,
Winter's breath forevermore.

Twirling flakes in a frosty swirl,
Nature's magic all around,
Every heart begins to twirl,
In this beauty, joy is found.

Candles glow in window frames,
Warmth that fights the winter chill,
A dance of shadows, flickering flames,
Embers of hope, spirits still.

Life endures in the crisp air,
Glimmers fade into the night,
Yet warmth lingers everywhere,
In winter's chill, hearts take flight.

Ethereal Lights Over Snowdrifts

Softly glowing in the night,
Ethereal lights begin to rise,
Draped in snow, a blanket white,
Underneath the velvet skies.

Each flake falls with a secret song,
Whirling softly to the ground,
A peaceful hush where dreams belong,
In stillness, magic can be found.

Winds carry whispers, secrets told,
Through the trees that stand in awe,
Of starlit nights and stories old,
Nature's beauty fills the raw.

Glimmers catch in hopeful eyes,
As shadows dance upon the snow,
In the stillness, wonder lies,
Each breath taken, soft and slow.

Memories linger in frozen air,
Ethereal moments crafted fine,
Wrapped in quiet, calm and rare,
In winter's grace, our hearts entwine.

Stellar Echoes in the Cold

Underneath a canopy vast,
Stellar echoes hum and glide,
Through the chill, their songs are cast,
A cosmic waltz, in stars we bide.

Frosty breath of the distant night,
Guides us through the endless flow,
Patterns twinkling, pure delight,
In the dark, soft pulses show.

Galaxies spin in rhythmic grace,
Silent wishes drift through space,
A tapestry of time and place,
Inherit the cosmos, we embrace.

In the coldest hour, still we seek,
Stellar whispers, tender and meek,
Carried forth, our spirits speak,
To the universe, our hearts unique.

Echoes of light in the frigid air,
Guiding us home, where dreams ignite,
Each starlit gleam, a prayer to share,
In tranquil awe beneath the night.

Cosmic Silhouettes Against Frost

Dark silhouettes against the snow,
Branches reach for the cosmos wide,
In winter's bite, we feel the glow,
Silent beauty, nature's pride.

Stars above like distant dreams,
Painting stories with their light,
In whispered secrets, nothing seems,
More alive than this serene night.

Frosted patterns trace the ground,
Every breath a cloud of mist,
In this calm, love can be found,
Held in whispers, none can resist.

As shadows stretch with evening's grace,
Cosmic wonders draw us near,
In each moment's tender embrace,
Winter's magic becomes clear.

Guided by the twinkling skies,
Against the frost, our dreams align,
In cosmic dance, our spirits rise,
In the night's embrace, we shine.

Whispers of Frosted Nights

In shadows deep, the cold winds sigh,
The moonlight dances, sparkling shy.
Whispers of frost upon the ground,
Silent secrets lost, yet found.

Bare branches cradle stars that gleam,
Frosted dreams in winter's theme.
The night enfolds with a tender touch,
A hush surrounds, it's felt so much.

Each breath a cloud, in the air it sways,
Through frosty paths, the heart obeys.
Echoes linger of the day gone by,
Under the watchful, starry sky.

In the stillness, a story unfolds,
Of whispered hopes and tales retold.
A canvas white, the earth adorned,
In frosted peace, the world is warmed.

As dawn approaches, the colors blend,
With hues so soft, the night must end.
But in the heart, those whispers stay,
A frosted night, that won't decay.

Celestial Snowfall

Slowly, gently, the snowflakes fall,
A blanket white, it covers all.
Stars above twinkle, cast their light,
In the stillness of the snowy night.

Each flake a whisper from the skies,
A soft embrace, a sweet surprise.
Glittering dreams dance on the breeze,
As winter's chill brings hearts to ease.

Luminous trails of silver glow,
Painting shadows beneath the snow.
In this silence, magic weaves,
A tapestry of hopes and dreams.

Gathered 'round, the world stands still,
In the snowy night, there's peace to fill.
The essence of love wrapped so tight,
In the embrace of a starry night.

With every flake that falls to ground,
New memories are quickly found.
In celestial snowfall, hearts ignite,
Under the canvas of endless night.

Dreams Beneath the Milky Way

Under the arch of celestial light,
Dreamers gather on this sacred night.
The Milky Way whispers sweetly low,
In the starlit tapestry's subtle glow.

With every twinkle, a wish takes flight,
Casting shadows, embracing the night.
Secrets linger in the clouds above,
As hearts entwine, guided by love.

Flowing like rivers of cosmic dust,
In dreams of starlight, we place our trust.
Through galaxies spinning, we drift away,
In the embrace of the Milky Way.

A lullaby hums from the depths of space,
As constellations align, we find our place.
In silent wonder, with every star,
We hold the universe, both near and far.

Beneath the canopy, we find our dreams,
As hope and magic glimmer and gleam.
A serenade played on cosmic strings,
In dreams beneath, our spirit sings.

Frost-Kissed Cosmos

In the quiet realm of a winter's night,
The cosmos glimmers, frosted bright.
Stars adorned with a crystal hue,
Invite our hearts to feel anew.

The night awakens with a gentle sigh,
As meteors streak across the sky.
Whispers echo from worlds apart,
Frost-kissed dreams warm the heart.

Through cosmic trails of shimmering light,
Magic dances, a wondrous sight.
With every breath, we draw the stars,
Feeling their glow, healing our scars.

The universe hums in a quiet embrace,
Each twinkle an echo of infinite grace.
In the stillness, our spirits soar,
In the frost-kissed cosmos, we dream once more.

Under the blanket of night so vast,
We weave our hopes, with shadows cast.
In the embrace of this celestial sea,
Frost-kissed cosmos, forever free.

Radiance in Falling Snow

Softly the snowflakes drift and sway,
Whispers of winter night display.
Each flake a story, pure and bright,
Laying a quilt under the soft moonlight.

The world becomes a canvas white,
Sparkling gems in the pale twilight.
Footsteps crunch in the silent air,
Nature's calm, a tranquil prayer.

Branches bow with a frosty crown,
Beauty embraced in the softest gown.
Winds carry laughter, crisp and rare,
Joyous echoes everywhere.

In this stillness, hearts find peace,
Moments linger, troubles cease.
Radiance glows in every flake,
In falling snow, we awake.

Underneath the starry spell,
Winter's magic weaves so well.
Every breath a frosty kiss,
In the calm, find eternal bliss.

Gleaming Silence

In the hush of night, whispers grow,
Gleaming silence, soft and slow.
Stars twinkle bright in the quiet sky,
Secrets and dreams gently float by.

Shadows dance with a soft embrace,
Moonlight spills in a silver lace.
Every shadow holds a tale,
In the stillness, we set sail.

Crickets sing with a muted sound,
Nature's symphony all around.
Each breath taken, serene and clear,
In the silence, we draw near.

Time stands still, as dreams take flight,
In the gleaming embrace of night.
Moments linger without a sound,
In the silence, love is found.

So let us wander, hand in hand,
Through sacred spaces, unplanned.
For in quietude, we ignite,
The heart's soft glow, where dreams unite.

Celestial Tales in the Cold

Beneath the blanket of starlit sky,
The cold winds whisper, a gentle sigh.
Celestial tales twinkle and weave,
In the heart of night, we believe.

Frozen lakes mirror the heavens above,
Embracing the stories of hope and love.
Each star a wish, shining so bold,
In the vast expanse, secrets unfold.

Clouds dance softly, draping the night,
Veils of frost that shimmer with light.
The cosmos sings of distant shores,
In every twinkle, the universe pours.

And as we stand in this cosmic embrace,
We trace the patterns of time and space.
With every breath, we set out to roam,
Finding in stars our eternal home.

So let the cold melt our fears away,
With celestial tales guiding the way.
In the night's embrace, dreams grow bold,
In the stories of winter, warmth is told.

Midnight's Frozen Whisper

In midnight's grasp, the world is still,
A frozen whisper, a gentle thrill.
Each star a beacon, a guiding light,
In shadows deep, dreams take flight.

The moon hangs low, a silver guide,
Illuminating secrets that we hide.
Silent echoes in the icy air,
Promises linger everywhere.

Frosted breath misting in the night,
Hearts entwine in a sacred rite.
We walk paths only fate can see,
In midnight's arms, we are free.

Every heartbeat syncs with the frost,
In this stillness, we find what's lost.
Let the night cradle our hopes anew,
With frozen whispers and dreams so true.

Lost in the magic of the dark embrace,
We trace constellations, a timeless space.
For in every silence, love will stir,
In midnight's whisper, it's just us, her.

Enchanted in Chill

In twilight's soft embrace, we stand,
The air is filled with magic's hand.
Whispers dance on the frozen breeze,
As dreams unfold beneath the trees.

Moonlit shadows waltz and sway,
Guiding us through the night's ballet.
Stars above in splendor gleam,
Casting spells on a midnight dream.

Frosted petals, silver bright,
Glowing softly in the night.
Each breath a cloud, a fleeting chill,
In this enchanted world, we will.

Nature sings in hushed refrain,
Echoes of the summer's reign.
Yet here in winter's charm we find,
A cozy warmth that binds the mind.

As icy fingers trace the ground,
In sparkling silence, peace is found.
With you, my heart begins to soar,
Enchanted in chill, forevermore.

The Moon's Icy Caress

Underneath the starry dome,
The moon sends shivers to our home.
Its icy caress, a gentle kiss,
Transforming night into pure bliss.

Glittering frost on every leaf,
Whispers soft, hinting of belief.
Echoes of a serene embrace,
In every shadow, a silvery trace.

Winds sing sweetly through the trees,
A haunting note upon the breeze.
The world adorned in crystal light,
Awakens magic in the night.

Each star a gem in the endless sea,
Tales of love and mystery.
The moon dips low with a tender glance,
Inviting dreamers to their dance.

When night unfolds its velvet hue,
In the midst of dreams, I find you.
The moon's embrace, forever near,
Whispers of hope that calms all fear.

Starshine on Crystal Seas

Beneath a sky of velvet blue,
Starshine glimmers, pure and true.
Upon the waves, a dance of light,
Guiding souls through the tranquil night.

Reflections shimmer, dreams take flight,
A world transformed by soft starlight.
Whispers of the ocean's call,
In rhythmic waves, we lose it all.

The breeze carries secrets from afar,
Each ripple sparkles like a star.
In this embrace, we drift away,
Where the past and present sway.

Navigating by celestial beams,
We sail through haunting midnight dreams.
In the stillness, hearts align,
In starshine's glow, forever mine.

Carried by the night's soft grace,
Time stands still in this sacred space.
With every tide, our spirits roam,
On crystal seas, we've found our home.

Night's Ethereal Tapestry

In the fabric of the night,
Dreams are woven, pure delight.
Threads of starlight intertwine,
Creating visions, yours and mine.

Each moment, a delicate stitch,
In this realm where thoughts enrich.
The moon, a needle, gently weaves,
As we embark on journeys achieved.

Whispers brush against the skin,
In this tapestry, where we begin.
Colors blend in a cosmic hue,
Painting visions just for you.

Through the veil of nighttime's grace,
We find solace in this place.
Echoes linger, soft and sweet,
In the dance where rhythms meet.

As dawn approaches with a sigh,
The tapestry fades but won't die.
For every night, a story spun,
A timeless thread, forever begun.

Tales from a Frosted Heaven

In a realm where silence reigns,
Snowflakes dance through soft refrains,
Echoes of a winter's breath,
Whispers of the dreams of death.

Crystals spark in pale moonlight,
Shimmering dreams take their flight,
Frozen echoes sing their song,
In this place where souls belong.

Silver trees with branches low,
Cradling secrets, soft and slow,
Each moment still, a sacred vow,
In the frost, we gather now.

Wanderers from far and wide,
Drift like shadows, none can hide,
In this realm of frosted grace,
We find truth in nature's face.

The night lifts, and dawn draws near,
Breaking chill with warmth sincere,
Tales from heaven, soft and free,
In frost, we find our unity.

Fables Woven in Frost

In the cradle of the cold,
Fables whispered, ages old,
Threads of silver interlace,
Time and stories leave their trace.

The icy winds bear secrets tight,
Crafted softly, pure delight,
In each flake, a tale unfolds,
Of forgotten dreams, retold.

Creatures slumber, dreams afloat,
In the stillness of the note,
Fables woven, soft and bright,
Glinting in the pale moonlight.

Underneath the frosty skies,
Hope and wonder gently rise,
Every story's bound to weave,
The magic we choose to believe.

Through the veil of crystal nights,
Hearts embrace the frozen sights,
Woven in the quilt of ice,
Fables shimmer, faith's device.

Whispers Under Frozen Stars

Beneath a shroud of velvet night,
Whispers drift in cold moonlight,
Stars alight like ancient dreams,
Glowing softly as time seems.

Among the shadows, stories bloom,
In the stillness, they consume,
Frozen stellar tales untold,
Of places warm, of hearts so bold.

Voices linger, soft and clear,
Every murmur sings of fear,
Underneath that cosmic gaze,
Life's fleeting, delicate ways.

In the silence, secrets lie,
Like a breath that will not die,
Whispers weave through starry night,
Wrapping dreams in silver light.

Hope ignites as dawn draws near,
Whispers fade, but hearts stay clear,
Under stars that tease and play,
Frozen tales never decay.

The Chill of Celestial Light

In the chill of silent grace,
Celestial dance, a slow embrace,
Galaxies twirl in a frozen waltz,
Painting shadows, time exalts.

Light cascades on snow-kissed ground,
Melodies of silence found,
Every glimmer tells a tale,
Of starry nights that never pale.

In the haze of icy dreams,
Life unfurling, softly gleams,
Echoes from the depths of space,
Bringing warmth to this cold place.

The cosmos breathes with tender care,
Frozen whispers fill the air,
In the chill, a warmth ignites,
Celestial wonders guide our sights.

As dusk fades, the twilight sighs,
Light retreats, yet never dies,
In the chill, our hearts take flight,
Awakening the celestial light.

Frosty Veil of Night

In the silent night so deep,
Frosty whispers gently creep.
Moonlight dances on the snow,
Casting shadows, soft and slow.

Trees adorned with icy lace,
Nature sleeps in a tranquil space.
Stars behold the world below,
Wrapped in winter's frosty glow.

Winds caress with a chilly breath,
Reminding all of nature's depth.
Underneath this silver dome,
Dreamers wander, far from home.

Every flake a work of art,
Crafted by a tender heart.
Night embraces every tree,
In its calm and quiet plea.

Frosty veils entwine the night,
In their beauty, pure delight.
As the world begins to rest,
In this stillness, we are blessed.

Shimmering Frostbites

Morning breaks in a golden haze,
Frostbites glimmer, a sparkling maze.
Each step crackles underfoot,
Nature's jewels in winter's suit.

Hues of blue and silver spark,
Artistry etched in every park.
The world dressed for a ball tonight,
Sparkling sharp in the soft daylight.

Whispers of chill linger near,
Beneath the frost, dreams appear.
Echoes dance in the frosted air,
A fleeting moment, rare and fair.

Crisp leaves flutter, a shimmery sight,
A crystalline quilt, so pure, so bright.
Under the sun's gentle kiss,
Winter's wonder, a fleeting bliss.

In the stillness, magic thrives,
Beauty in each frost that survives.
Shimmering tales of ice unfold,
In winter's arms, a story told.

The Velvet Touch of Stars

Twinkling gems in the velvet sky,
Whispering dreams that float nearby.
With each glance, hearts ignite,
In the embrace of endless night.

Softly shining, they seem to weave,
Stories that we long to believe.
A tapestry of light and grace,
Guiding us to a sacred place.

In the quiet of midnight's glow,
Stars unveil what we long to know.
Secrets sleeping in the deep,
Nurtured by the cosmos's keep.

Eyes closed tight, we reach so far,
Breathing in the light of stars.
Each twinkle a silent prayer,
Bridge to the wonders hidden there.

The velvet touch sends us to dream,
Floating on a celestial stream.
In the dark, our spirits soar,
Finding peace forever more.

Quiet Radiance Above

Above the world, a soft light glows,
In the stillness, a secret flows.
Clouds drift softly, painted gray,
Cradling sunlight, fading away.

From twilight's hush, the stars cascade,
Illuminating the night's parade.
Glimmers flicker, a gentle sigh,
Hearts awaken as shadows fly.

Moonbeams dance on the quiet ground,
In their embrace, calmness is found.
Whispers travel through the air,
Tell of dreams and lingered care.

Each moment held in tender light,
Bathing us in magic bright.
An embrace that speaks so true,
Quiet radiance shines anew.

As the world slows its busy race,
In this glow, we find our place.
Under the vast celestial dome,
We gather peace, we find our home.

The Night's Shimmering Awakenings

Beneath the moon's soft glow,
Whispers dance on frosty air,
Stars awaken dreams untold,
In the night, magic lays bare.

Silent shadows weave and twine,
Every breath a fleeting sigh,
Hope reborn with every shine,
As the night begins to fly.

Crickets chirp a soft melody,
Nature's pulse hums through the trees,
Awakening the mysteries,
On a breeze that gently frees.

A silver path of glistening light,
Leads to realms we long to find,
Each step whispers tales of night,
As the stars begin to bind.

In this hour, hearts interlace,
Joined by dreams both strong and pure,
In the shimmering night's embrace,
We find peace, we find our cure.

Lost in a Frosted Reverie

The world wrapped in icy sheets,
A dreamscape of silent white,
Footprints lie where moments greet,
In the magic of the night.

Frosted whispers kiss the trees,
Nature's breath in crystal form,
Shattering the stillness, ease,
In winter's quiet, we are warm.

Every flake a story spun,
In each crystal, secrets swirl,
Lost in dreams till day is done,
Winter's dance begins to twirl.

Moonlit paths we wander slow,
Wrapped in the chill's embrace,
With every step, our spirits grow,
In the cold, we find our place.

In this frosted reverie's glow,
Our hearts ignite with gentle fire,
Lost yet found, we ebb and flow,
Carried forth on winter's choir.

Starlit Dreams on a Frozen Path

Through the night, we wander wide,
On a path of glistening snow,
Stars above like diamonds ride,
Guiding dreams where wonders flow.

Each step forward, shimmers bright,
Whispers spill from every tree,
In the calm of this cold night,
Endless skies set our hearts free.

Softly, softly, breathless air,
Paints the world in silvery hues,
In this stillness, we declare,
Every moment, ours to choose.

Frozen beams of light at play,
Lead us on through twilight's grace,
In starlit dreams, we gently sway,
Finding solace in this space.

With hearts alight, our spirits blend,
Dancing shadows join the song,
In this dream, our souls transcend,
On a frozen path, we belong.

Aura of the Winter Night

In the hush of winter's breath,
An aura drapes the sleeping earth,
Silent whispers cradle death,
Yet bring forth a quiet rebirth.

Stars wink softly through the frost,
A symphony of chill delights,
In the shadowed woods, we're lost,
Underneath the glittering sights.

Each flake falls like a secret sigh,
Wrapping dreams in purest white,
The heart feels light as time drifts by,
In the depths of winter's night.

Glimmers of hope in the darkness weave,
Threads of warmth through needles cold,
In this magic, we believe,
Tales of winter gently told.

Under the moon, we seek to find,
An aura bright that lingers near,
As our souls in silence bind,
Winter's charm, forever clear.

The Dance of Snowflakes and Stars

Snowflakes twirl in the night sky,
Gently falling from above.
Stars wink as they dance nearby,
Whispers of a silent love.

Each flake a spark of pure grace,
Painting dreams in the cold air.
They weave a tale in their free space,
A ballet of beauty so rare.

Moonlight casts shadows so bright,
Guiding the flight of each flake.
They shimmer like jewels in the light,
A magical world they create.

In this ballet, time seems to freeze,
As winter's breath takes its hold.
The heart finds peace, a gentle ease,
In the wonders of stories untold.

So let us dance with the snowflakes,
Beneath the vast, starlit sea.
For in this moment, joy awakes,
A timeless, enchanting spree.

A Canvas of Ice and Light

The lake is a canvas, smooth and bright,
Reflecting the dance of the day.
Crystals glimmer in beams of white,
Nature's art on display.

Brushstrokes of frost paint the trees,
Each branch adorned with a crown.
Whispers of winter in the breeze,
As sun bids the shadows drown.

Icicles hang like chandeliers,
Sparkling under a sapphire sky.
With every glint, it draws us near,
To pause, to wonder, to sigh.

Footprints march on this frozen stream,
In a dance of laughter and play.
Capturing moments, like a dream,
In winter's gentle sway.

Let's celebrate this icy delight,
A masterpiece in every view.
In a world where day meets night,
Each scene a vision, forever new.

Dreaming Under Cosmos

Beneath the quilt of endless night,
We gather under a starlit dome.
Galaxies swirl, a wondrous sight,
In this vast celestial home.

Whispers of dreams ride the lunar beams,
As constellations tell their tales.
The universe hums with silent themes,
Where imagination never fails.

We lay on grass, our hearts aligned,
Gazing at infinity's sprawl.
Time loses meaning, thoughts unwind,
In this ethereal, cosmic hall.

Shooting stars like wishes soar,
Each twinkle a secret to share.
We long for more, forever explore,
In the magic that lingers in air.

As dawn approaches, dreams gently fade,
Yet hope in our hearts will reside.
Under the cosmos, memories made,
In the universe, we confide.

Chilling Constellations

In the heart of winter's chill,
Constellations glimmer bright.
Each star a promise, a silent thrill,
Illuminating the cold night.

The Big Dipper spills its glow,
A guiding hand for those astray.
While Orion's belt, a tale of woe,
Shimmers in the solar ballet.

Frosty nights unveil their might,
As we seek warmth in dreams spun.
A cosmos alive, a dazzling sight,
Where stories weave and hopes run.

We gather close in the frosty air,
Wrapped in blankets, hearts aglow.
In the laughter shared, we cast our cares,
As the universe sings low.

Through chilly nights and stardust skies,
We find connection in the cold.
Underneath vast, twinkling ties,
The dreams of the night unfold.

Silver Threads of Dusk

Whispers weave through twilight air,
Soft shadows dance, a gentle pair.
The sky dons hues of deepening gray,
As silver threads lead night to play.

A tranquil hush falls over the land,
Fingers entwined, we understand.
Stars begin to peek and gleam,
In this moment, we share a dream.

The world transforms in dusky light,
With each heartbeat, darkness takes flight.
Fading sun, a final bow,
Embracing night, here, and now.

Memories stir in the fading glow,
A soft serenade begins to flow.
Each note a promise of the dark,
A quiet lullaby, a spark.

Let silver threads guide our way,
Through endless night until the day.
Together we'll wander, hand in hand,
On silver threads, we'll softly stand.

The Night Sky's Embrace

Underneath the velvet dome,
The stars invite us to roam.
Crickets sing a soft refrain,
In the night, we lose our pain.

Moonlight drapes like silk so fine,
Whispering secrets, intertwine.
The world below lulled in sleep,
While the heavens joyfully leap.

Galaxies swirl in distant grace,
Each twinkle holds a warm embrace.
Constellations tell their tales,
As silence wraps, and wonder prevails.

Stardust glimmers on our skin,
A quiet invitation within.
Here in stillness, dreams ignite,
Beneath the endless, watchful night.

Let us weave our hopes up high,
Into the depths of the sky.
For in the night, our spirits soar,
The sky's embrace forevermore.

Glimmers of the Frozen Expanse

In the stillness, frosted breath,
Cold beauty mingles with sweet death.
Crystals sparkle on every tree,
Glimmers of magic, wild and free.

A blanket white, the world adorns,
As morning wakes and beauty warns.
Every whisper, a shiver of ice,
In this expanse, the heart feels nice.

Breath of winter, crisp and clear,
Echoing softly, drawing near.
Footprints trail through endless glow,
Where time stands still in the snow.

Ancient tales in whispers told,
Glimmers of silver, purest gold.
Nature's heart in frozen state,
Inviting us to meditate.

In every flake, a story spun,
A fleeting moment, swiftly done.
In this expanse, we find our place,
With glimmers bright, in winter's grace.

Twinkling Above the Frozen Plains

The plains stretch wide, a canvas white,
Adorned with twinkling stars so bright.
A hush blankets the chilly ground,
In every shadow, dreams are found.

Moonbeams dance on glistening hills,
Whispers carried by winter's thrills.
Each star a guide, a sparkling friend,
Leading us where the night may end.

Across the sky, a canvas drawn,
A tapestry of twilight's dawn.
We chase the light on frozen ground,
In silent beauty, we are bound.

Each step we take, the world awakes,
In twinkling light, the heart quakes.
The frozen plains tell tales anew,
Under the stars, a world so true.

As night drapes softly over all,
In twinkling beauty, we stand tall.
Above the frozen plains we gaze,
In endless wonder, our hearts ablaze.

Serene Echoes of Night

The moonlight whispers soft and low,
Casting dreams where shadows flow.
Stars twinkle like a distant sigh,
In the arms of night, we lie.

Gentle breezes carry tales untold,
Of ancient paths and secrets bold.
A lullaby of silence we seek,
In the tranquil dark, we speak.

The tranquil water reflects the sky,
Rippling thoughts as time slips by.
Each echo dances in the calm,
Wrapping our hearts in a soothing balm.

Nighttime holds its tender grace,
In every moment, we find our place.
With every star, a wish takes flight,
In the soothing arms of the night.

Here we find our silent mirth,
In the gentle hush of birth.
Serene echoes cradle our dreams,
In the night, life softly gleams.

Enigmas in the Frost

Morning dawns with a crystal hue,
Whispers of frost, a world anew.
Nature dons her icy crown,
Enigmas swirl as the sunlight frowns.

Footsteps crunch on a carpet white,
Mysteries dance in the morning light.
Fractals sparkle, a ghostly sheet,
Unraveling tales beneath our feet.

Trees wear coats of shimmering lace,
A fleeting moment, an ethereal space.
Each breath, a cloud in the biting air,
Life pauses, caught in frozen prayer.

Hidden truths in the frigid air,
Secrets held with delicate care.
Frost-kissed whispers beckon us near,
To ponder wonders year after year.

A world transformed, so breathtaking,
In frozen beauty, our hearts are waking.
With every sigh, we're drawn to seek,
The enigmas in the frost, unique.

Dance of the Winter Lights

Stars ignite in the velvet sky,
A cosmic waltz where dreams can fly.
Winter's breath spins tales of old,
In shimmering splendor, a sight to behold.

Dancing shadows paint the ground,
With every flicker, magic found.
The chill air crackles, alive with cheer,
As winter lights draw us near.

Let the snowflakes twirl and play,
In the tender glow of the moon's ballet.
Each sparkle whispers secrets bright,
In the radiant dance of the night.

Embers of warmth in the icy breeze,
Stir the heart, put the mind at ease.
A festival of lights ignites our soul,
Binding us in a luminous whole.

In this dance, our spirits soar,
With winter's grace, we explore.
Through the fleeting moments we find,
A magic that lingers in heart and mind.

The Hush of Sparkling Night

Beneath the stars, a silence reigns,
Whispers of night weave through the plains.
The world is draped in a cloak so bright,
In the gentle hush of sparkling night.

Crickets chirp a lullaby sweet,
While fireflies twinkle, a dance discreet.
Each glimmer holds a secret sigh,
That floats through the dark, like a gentle high.

Clouds drift slowly with silver threads,
Painting shadows where the night spreads.
A canvas of dreams, pure and light,
Awash in the hush of the starry night.

Moments linger, time stands still,
As the heart drinks deep of the night's thrill.
Under the blanket of stars so bright,
We find our peace in the sparkling night.

With every breath, the magic grows,
In silent realms where the starlight glows.
Together we cherish these dreams in flight,
In the embrace of the sparkling night.

Celestial Ornaments in the Snow

Beneath the moon's soft glow,
Sparkling snowflakes dance below,
Their light, like diamonds cast,
Whispers of winter's gentle past.

Each flake a story told,
Mirrors of beauty, bright and bold,
Adorning the world in pure delight,
Crafting a wonderland of white.

Branches bow with snowy dress,
Nature's art in quietness,
A tapestry of dreams unfurled,
Celestial ornaments grace the world.

In twilight's hush, magic sways,
A serene peace in winter's ways,
The stars above blink and wink,
As we embrace this frozen ink.

With every step, the crunch of bliss,
Winter's charm we can't dismiss,
Wrapped in warmth, we take our flight,
Beneath ornaments of white.

A Symphony of Winter's Glow

In the hush of falling snow,
Nature plays a soft piano,
Each flake a note, a gentle sound,
Harmonies in silence abound.

The wind whispers, a soothing breeze,
Trees sway gently, dance with ease,
Underneath the starlit sky,
Winter sings, as time slips by.

Footsteps crunch on pristine trails,
Echoes of laughter, joy prevails,
A symphony of frosty air,
Wrapped in warmth, we breathe and share.

Icicles glint like silver strings,
Carrying whispers of secret things,
The world a canvas, painted bright,
A symphony of winter's light.

As day fades and shadows blend,
We gather close, with hearts to mend,
Creating memories in the snow,
A winter glow, forever aglow.

Celestial Ocean of Snowflakes

Waves of white cascade and flow,
A celestial ocean, soft and slow,
Snowflakes drift like gentle dreams,
In winter's embrace, the world redeems.

Each flake descends, a silent song,
Carpeting earth where we belong,
A vast expanse, serene and pure,
In this ocean, our souls endure.

The sky blushes with hues of night,
Stars peek through, twinkling bright,
With every breath, we feel the chill,
A moment of peace, a gentle thrill.

Together we wander, hand in hand,
In this vast, enchanting land,
With laughter echoing near and far,
We dance beneath the evening star.

As dawn approaches, colors collide,
The ocean sparkles, a snowy tide,
In this winter wonder, hearts find grace,
In the celestial ocean, our place.

Chasing Winter Stars

In the stillness of night, we roam,
Chasing stars, we feel at home,
Under blankets of velvet sky,
Winter's breath sings softly by.

Frosted air, a crystalline bite,
Guides our steps through the silent white,
Heartbeats echo, a rhythmic trance,
In this magic, we dare to dance.

Footprints left in shimmering snow,
Tales we tell and laughter flows,
In the glow of the moon so bright,
Chasing stars that pierce the night.

Together we wander, dreams alight,
Starlit wishes take their flight,
With every breath, the world stands still,
As we chase winter's beauty at will.

When dawn arrives, we bid adieu,
To winter stars that fade from view,
But in our hearts, they ever remain,
Guiding our joy through snow and rain.

Starlit Trails on Winter's Breath

Beneath the sky, the stars align,
Whispers of dreams in the chill combine.
Snowflakes dance on the velvet night,
Guiding the heart with soft, pure light.

Footprints trace a path so bright,
Echoes of laughter, pure delight.
In the hush of night, time stands still,
Wrapped in warmth, a magical thrill.

Fires crackle, warmth we share,
Stories woven in the frosty air.
Love ignites beneath the moon,
Drawing us closer, a tender tune.

Wandering souls on nature's crest,
Feel the peace, a gentle rest.
With every breath, the winter sings,
A serenade of cherished things.

The world is hushed, a sweet embrace,
In starlit trails, we find our place.
With winter's breath, our spirits soar,
Together we cherish forevermore.

Ephemeral Glow of January

In January's arms, time stands still,
With whispers of frost on the windowsill.
Moments fleeting, a flickering flame,
Life's fragile beauty, never the same.

Morning light spills on pristine snow,
Painting each branch with a gentle glow.
Footsteps mark paths in the silence wide,
Echoes of winter, our hearts' guide.

Dreams like snowflakes, unique in flight,
Drifting on breezes, soft and light.
In the embrace of the chilly air,
We find our solace, a bond to share.

The dusky dusk brings a tranquil hue,
While the stars awaken, bright and new.
A tapestry woven of light and shade,
In January's glow, our hopes cascade.

As the days stretch, we hold on tight,
To fleeting glimmers that shine so bright.
With every heartbeat, the world turns bold,
In the ephemeral glow, a story told.

Frosted Wishes Amidst Nightfall

When night descends, the world feels still,
Frosted wishes dance with a quiet thrill.
Crystals of ice catch the moonlit gleam,
Whispers of hope in a starlit dream.

Each wish a star in the deep azure,
Floating on breezes, tender and pure.
Cold embraces wrap us tight,
As we gather 'round the firelight.

Voices softer in the winter's breath,
Speaking of love, the warmth of depth.
With each crackle, stories unfold,
Treasured memories in the night cold.

Beneath the blanket of velvet skies,
We paint our dreams with fervent sighs.
In the magic of nightfall's kiss,
Frosted wishes find their bliss.

As we linger, hearts intertwined,
Finding solace, the stars aligned.
With every glance, a promise made,
In frosted wishes, love won't fade.

Celestial Hues in a Winter's Dream

In a winter's dream, celestial hues,
Paint the landscape with vibrant views.
Where azure skies meet snowy plains,
Nature whispers softly in gentle refrains.

Amidst the stillness, peace is found,
As stars sprinkle light on the frozen ground.
Icicles hang like crystal art,
Reflecting the magic of every heart.

Footprints traverse the frosty ground,
Echoes of joy in laughter are found.
Snowflakes twirl like dancers at play,
In a world transformed, they drift away.

The moon shines bright, casting its spell,
In the cold embrace, we know it well.
With every heartbeat, we feel alive,
In winter's wonder, our spirits thrive.

As dawn breaks softly, the colors bloom,
Carried by whispers from night's sweet gloom.
In celestial hues, we find our scheme,
A canvas of beauty in winter's dream.

Star-Cloaked Serenity

In the quiet dusk, stars gleam bright,
Whispers of dreams take flight.
Night wraps the world in a loving embrace,
Serenity glows on the cosmic face.

Beneath the vast, unfurling sky,
The hearts of wanderers softly sigh.
In the hush, hope's gentle call,
Echoes of peace, nurturing all.

Silver beams dance on tranquil seas,
Carrying secrets on the breeze.
Each twinkling light, a story told,
Of ancient souls, brave and bold.

In soft shadows, thoughts entwine,
Hearts warm like a vintage wine.
Finding solace in the night's glow,
In star-cloaked serenity, love will flow.

As dawn approaches, stars'll fade away,
Yet their light stays, come what may.
In memories held, they softly gleam,
In the heart's quiet, they still dream.

On Frosted Wings

Whispers of winter on the breeze,
Fluttering softly through the trees.
Each flake falls with grace and charm,
Warming hearts with their chilly balm.

On frosted wings, a world reborn,
Silence weaves the fabric of morn.
Footprints linger in the snow,
Stories of warmth in winter's glow.

Underneath the pale moon's light,
Dreamers wander into the night.
Each breath, a puff of frosty air,
Encasing wishes, light as fair.

Embers dance in the hearth's embrace,
Filling shadows in every space.
Time slows down, a gentle kiss,
In the chill, we find our bliss.

On frosted wings, hope takes flight,
Guided by dreams through the night.
With every dawn, the sun will sing,
Of joy and warmth that spring will bring.

The Night's Crystal Heart

In the depths of twilight's spell,
A crystal heart begins to swell.
Holding whispers, secrets dear,
The night stands still, crystal clear.

Stars like diamonds, glowing bright,
Mark the path of soft moonlight.
Threads of silver softly weave,
In dreams that linger, hearts believe.

The cool breeze dances through the trees,
Carrying laughter and memories.
In shadows deep, love finds its way,
Guiding souls till break of day.

In the embrace of night's delight,
Fear fades into the soft twilight.
With every heartbeat, magic grows,
In the night's crystal heart, love flows.

And when dawn breaks the gentle call,
The heart stays warm, embracing all.
In every sunrise, hope will gleam,
Carried forth on the wings of dreams.

Cold Lullabies in the Dim

A hush blankets the world in dim,
Frosty whispers, soft and slim.
Stars hum very quiet tunes,
Underneath the watchful moons.

Cold lullabies brush the night,
Cradling dreams, devoid of fright.
In this haven, shadows play,
Wishing the worries far away.

Every sigh becomes a song,
Entwined in echoes that belong.
Frost-kissed air wraps around tight,
Guarding souls till morning light.

In the stillness, hearts can rest,
Nestled deep, feeling blessed.
Calm as winter's gentle hand,
Cradling dreams like grains of sand.

Through the veil of chilling night,
Lullabies bring the heart to light.
In the cold, warmth will bloom,
In the dim, love finds room.

Mysteries in the Winter Glow

Snowflakes whisper secrets soft,
illuminated by the moon's gentle croft.
Shadows dance in twilight's sigh,
as winter holds its breath and nigh.

The chill air breathes a tale untold,
wrapped in blankets of silver and gold.
Pine trees guard the silent night,
under stars that shimmer bright.

Footprints trace a story clear,
of laughter shared and warmth near.
Each step a note in nature's song,
where hearts entwine and belong.

The world transformed in frosty lace,
a serene and peaceful space.
Glowing embers in the fireplace,
where memories find a warm embrace.

Mysteries linger in every flake,
woven softly, the silence we take.
Winter's canvas, pure and bright,
invites us to dream in the night.

Reflections of Ice and Light

In the stillness, shadows gleam,
frozen whispers, a captured dream.
Mirrors of ice beneath the sky,
hold the secrets of days gone by.

Sunlight dances on crystal's edge,
painting colors in a sparkling pledge.
Each glint and shimmer tells a tale,
carried softly on the winter gale.

Rippling waters, a silvery thread,
weave through the frost and the clear white bed.
Nature's art, a masterpiece bright,
draped in layers of pure delight.

In every step on this icy ground,
echoes of laughter can still be found.
Moment's reflections in icy sights,
dance like stars on velvet nights.

Unseen realms live within this chill,
where time slows down against its will.
Embrace the beauty, hold it tight,
in the reflections of ice and light.

The Dance of Distant Stars

In the velvet of night, they gleam,
distant dreams stitched within a seam.
Each flicker tells a tale of old,
of journeys taken, brave and bold.

The cosmos sways in rhythmic flight,
a ballet of wonders, pure delight.
Nebulas swirl in vibrant hues,
painting the dark with cosmic views.

Sighs of comets brush the sky,
leaving trails of magic as they fly.
Planets whisper secrets soft,
carved by time in the vast loft.

Each star becomes a guiding light,
leading hearts through the endless night.
We dance beneath their endless glow,
as dreams awaken and softly flow.

The universe sings a lullaby,
cradling wishes as they drift by.
In the dance of distant stars we find,
a bond unbroken, forever entwined.

Frosty Kisses from Above

Gentle flakes fall from the sky,
like whispered words, they float and fly.
Each frosty kiss a sweet embrace,
softening edges in time and space.

Trees stand tall, adorned in white,
guardians of the silent night.
Each branch cradles a shimmering dream,
wrapped in winter's quiet theme.

The world is hushed, a tranquil sight,
blanketed in the glow of light.
Chilled breaths linger as we roam,
finding solace far from home.

Laughter sparkles in the crisp, cool air,
as we twirl without a care.
Frosty kisses, a playful tease,
dancing softly with the winter breeze.

In every flake, a love bestowed,
memories weave in laughter glowed.
Frosty kisses from above we cherish,
in this winter wonder, let worries perish.

Reflections in the Winter Sky

Beneath a quilt of silver light,
The world lies still, a hush in night.
Stars like diamonds softly gleam,
Mirrored in the frosty stream.

Whispers dance on bitter air,
As memories swirl without a care.
Cold breaths linger, softly sigh,
With every gaze to winter's sky.

A silhouette in quietude,
Nature's peace, a haunting mood.
The moon, a guardian so high,
Guides the night with tender eye.

Trees dressed in frosted lace,
Stand as sentinels in this place.
Branches cradle dreams anew,
Reflecting hopes in crystal blue.

Beneath the canopy of dark,
Each snowflake finds its fleeting mark.
In this moment, time stands still,
In winter's grace, we find our will.

Echoes of the Night's Whisper

In the silence where shadows dwell,
Whispers breathe like a gentle bell.
Moonlight spills on the quiet ground,
Soft secrets linger all around.

Rustling leaves share their tales,
While the night wind gently sails.
Stars above weave a silver thread,
Connecting dreams to what lies ahead.

A distant call, a night bird's song,
Echoes float where the night feels long.
With every note, the darkness sways,
In unseen rhythms, softly plays.

Footsteps light on dewy grass,
As fleeting moments come to pass.
Each heartbeat fades in the night,
Lost in the hush, out of sight.

The heavens stretch, an endless sea,
In this expanse, we feel so free.
With every breath, we intertwine,
In echoes soft, our souls align.

Shimmers Against the Darkness

In the depths where shadows grow,
Tiny sparks begin to glow.
Flickers dance in the cold embrace,
Illuminating a secret space.

Each shimmer tells a quiet tale,
Of hopes that rise, of dreams that sail.
Against the dark, they light the path,
Breaking through the aftermath.

As night unfolds with velvet grace,
Stars emerge in a timeless chase.
Glimmers spark the endless night,
Carving paths of dazzling light.

In tender moments, quiet sighs,
Wonders weave between our eyes.
For every flicker, a wish is shared,
In the dark, we find we're cared.

Through velvet skies and shimmering seas,
Hope ignites on whispered breeze.
As shadows dance, so do we,
In every shimmer, we are free.

Illuminated by the Icy Sky

In the chill of a winter's night,
Stars ignite, a stunning sight.
The icy sky begins to glow,
As dreams awaken, soft and slow.

Moonlit shadows paint the ground,
In this hush, no other sounds.
White frosts whisper on the trees,
Each breath mingles with the breeze.

Crystals sparkle like scattered pearls,
As time around us gently swirls.
Each moment glistens, pure and bright,
In the embrace of the frozen night.

A tapestry of silvery grace,
Encircles us in soft embrace.
Underneath this vast expanse,
We lose ourselves in winter's dance.

Guided by the stars so near,
In this stillness, there is no fear.
Together, hearts in the icy air,
Find warmth in love's gentle care.

www.ingramcontent.com/pod-product-compliance
Ingram Content Group UK Ltd.
Pitfield, Milton Keynes, MK11 3LW, UK
UKHW031942151224
452382UK00006B/183

9 789916 798850